Whiskey for the Soul

by

Andre "Dre" Marshall

Copyright © 2024 by MANSA Project Solutions.

All rights reserved. No part of this publication may be reproduced, distributed, or transmitted in any form or by any means, including photocopying, recording, or other electronic or mechanical methods, without the prior written permission of the publisher, except in the case of brief quotations embodied in critical reviews and certain other non-commercial uses permitted by copyright law.

For permission requests, contact the publisher at:
MANSA Project Solutions

connect@mansaprojectsolutions.com
(904) 913-7689

www.mansaprojectsolutions.com
ISBN: 9798218547578

First Edition
Published by MANSA Project Solutions
Printed in the USA

Cover Design by Andre "Dre" Marshall

Disclaimer:

This book is a collection of thoughts, ideas, and quotes intended to motivate and inspire. While the content draws from various sources and personal experiences, it should not be interpreted as professional advice. The author, Andre "Dre" Marshall, and the publisher, MANSA Project Solutions, have made every effort to ensure accuracy, but make no claims or guarantees about the applicability or completeness of the content for every individual situation. Readers are encouraged to reflect on and interpret the ideas in their own way.The author and publisher assume no responsibility for any consequences arising from the use of this material.

To Charyse, my muse—your love sharpens my vision.

Jazmyn, AJ, Elle—your strength and spirit fuel my every step.

Mom, thank you for instilling relentless work ethic and unwavering faith.

To my family, friends, and mentors—your wisdom and support are the quiet forces behind every win.

And to everyone reading, I hope this book offers you something valuable on your journey.

The Spark

I didn't set out to write a book. This isn't about telling you how to live your life or pretending I've got all the answers. It's a collection of things I've learned through my own ups and downs, successes, failures, and everything in between. These are just things I've picked up while navigating life—nothing complicated, just a mix of what worked and what didn't. Some of these ideas came to me in the middle of conversations with friends, others while I was sitting alone at home, or after a long day in the studio. Often, the best lessons hit you when you least expect them, and I wanted to capture that here. It's raw, unfiltered, and practical—because life doesn't come with instructions, and sometimes, we just need someone to keep it real. When business took a hit during COVID, I was left questioning everything. Things semi-recovered but eventually fell through. I was stuck between trying to decide if I should keep going in music, drive Uber, or pack up and head to Thailand to become a philanthropist. It wasn't the big lessons that helped me through that—it was the simple quotes and thoughts that stuck with me, giving me the jolt I needed to take the next step. While I was building my new creative consulting company, MANSA Project Solutions, I knew I'd keep coaching creatives and business owners of all kinds. So, I started putting together the quotes and thoughts that I found myself leaning on regularly. I never planned for it to turn into a book, but here we are. I don't drink much anymore, but I used to appreciate how a shot of whiskey could give you that courage or confidence to take the next step.

That's what this book is meant to do—share a little courage, a little "whiskey," so you can take the next step, too. Whether you're grinding to build something big, or just trying to stay focused on the day-to-day, these pages are here to give you that push, that reminder: **You've got this.**

Opening Perspective

If you're reading this foreword, congrats—you're already a pro at procrastination. Seriously. You picked up a book packed with motivational quotes to fuel your entrepreneurial journey, and instead of diving headfirst into the inspiration, you're hanging out here, reading the foreword. That pause, that moment of looking ahead before you leap—that's exactly the kind of foresight you'll need to succeed. While others might rush in blindly, you're taking a moment to assess the landscape. That's where vision is born—right there in the pause before the plunge. This book isn't just a collection of motivational quotes; it's a playbook for the hustle. In a world that demands instant success, Dre's insights remind you that real progress takes time, grit, and vision. Now, I know what you're thinking. "Great, another quote book. I could just Google some quotes and call it a day." Let me stop you right there. This isn't just a collection of one-liners you're going to slap on Instagram with a fire emoji. These quotes have grit. They come from someone who's been in the trenches of the music industry, fought his way through, and came out the other side with battle scars —and success. They aren't just words on a page; they're a rallying cry for anyone who's ever had a dream and needed a reminder that it's okay to get knocked down if you get back up. You see, entrepreneurship isn't for the faint of heart. It's not glamorous, despite what social media will tell you. It's not a bunch of yacht parties and VIP sections. It's sleepless nights, unreturned calls, deals that fall through, and people who say, "Nah, that's not gonna work." Let me tell you what Dre Marshall would say to that: "Watch me." Because that's the mindset you need to succeed. You have to be ready to prove every doubter wrong, but more importantly, you have to prove to yourself that you have what it takes. I count myself incredibly fortunate to call Dre Marshall a friend, because witnessing his brilliance, vision, and relentless passion up close is nothing short of inspiring. I've had the privilege of watching not only his own journey but also the meteoric rise of those he's mentored and the clients fortunate enough to work with him. His ability to elevate others is something rare and powerful. In my life, there's a very small, trusted circle of people whose advice I hold in the highest regard—and Dre is one of them. If you can't have Dre on speed dial to call for guidance, then this book is the next best thing. Consider it your personal lifeline to the same wisdom and insight that has propelled so many to success. This book is for the dreamers and the doers, the grinders and the go-getters. It's for those of you who aren't just looking for success but are willing to chase it down and wrestle it into submission. Dre's quotes aren't just for reading—they're for living. They're for the moments when you feel like giving up, for the days when the world feels too heavy, and for the nights when your dream feels just out of reach. I promise you there will be days and nights like this.

Here's a secret they don't teach: entrepreneurship doesn't always feel good. In fact, a lot of the time, it's downright hard. Sometimes, it is so hard to succeed, if feels almost impossible. But you know what? Hard is where the magic happens. Hard is where you learn what you're made of, and hard is where you begin to build your empire. Success isn't about being the smartest or the most talented; it's about resilience. It's about having the guts to keep going when every sign flashes "turn back." It's about learning from the losses, not just celebrating the wins. Dre's about the real hustle—the kind where you're up before the sun and grinding long after the city lights have gone dim. He's been there, done that, and got the Grammy award and tons of other accolades to prove it. But what's more important? He remembers the grind, and that's where you come in. Now, this book you're holding in your hands (or scrolling on your device) is a gift from a man who knows a thing or two about hustling. Dre Marshall isn't just a name in the music industry—he's a force of nature. Dre's been around long enough to have seen every kind of ambition crash and burn, he knows what works and what doesn't and always helps people rise from the ashes, usually while dropping a sick beat. Everyone who is anyone in his industry knows Dre. Let these words push you out of your comfort zone and into the realm of possibility. Take these quotes he carefully curated and expounded upon, stick the best ones in your proverbial back pocket, and pull them out when the road gets rough. Because trust me, it will. But Dre's been there, and he's laid down this blueprint to help you find your way. Success isn't a straight path. It's more like attempting to sketch a perfect circle with your non-dominant hand after downing five shots of whiskey—messy, unpredictable, and a bit wobbly, but with enough persistence, it still gets done. You won't find any glittery platitudes in this book that suggest you can "manifest" your way to success JUST by thinking hard enough. Dre's more about telling you the hard truth: "You've got to work like you owe somebody money" because, spoiler alert, you probably do. If that doesn't resonate with you yet, it will after your first few months of entrepreneurship. Dre's also going to hit you with the good stuff, the kind of wisdom that makes you pause, reflect, and then shout, "Why didn't I think of that?!" He's been where you are, probably even worse off at some point, and yet here he is—living proof that you can not only survive in the shark-infested waters of entrepreneurship but thrive.

Dre's success is no accident. His story is like a mixtape of hustle, heart, and a whole lot of "no sleep 'til Brooklyn" vibes. That's the kind of energy you need to tap into if you want to make it as an entrepreneur. You've got to be ready to fail, then fail again, and then fail even harder—until, finally, that sweet moment of success arrives. Although Dre is a juggernaut in the music industry , this book isn't just for young entrepreneurs in the music industry. It's for anyone who's ever thought, "What if?" It's for anyone who's stared at a blank canvas and wondered what to create. It's for those who see opportunity where others see obstacles. And most importantly, it's for those who aren't afraid to fail, because failure is just another step toward success. Dre Marshall has walked this path, and now he's handing you the keys to unlock your own potential. The road won't be easy, but as you flip through these pages, I hope you realize something important that Dre and I know. If we can do it, so can you. Consider this your invitation to the Dre Marshall Hustle Academy. Enrollment is free, but the cost is your ego, your comfort zone, and maybe that idea you thought was the next big thing but is actually just the 12th version of something no one wants to buy. You'll come out the other side smarter, sharper, and—if all goes well —much wealthier. Here's my final tip: Don't just read this book—live it. Every quote, every page, every nugget of advice is fuel for your entrepreneurial rocket ship. Remember that no one cares if you've got a great rocket if you don't know how to launch it. Dre's been launching for years, and this is your backstage pass to see how it's done. Go get 'em, future mogul. I am rooting for you.

Sincerely,

Dr. Robert Urban

Entrepreneur | 6 Time Best-Selling Author | Founder/CEO of PaperBoat

What To Expect

This book is for anyone on the grind—whether you're calling the shots in the boardroom or making moves in the street. From CEOs to creatives, entrepreneurs to everyday hustlers, these pages offer real, practical lessons to help you stay sharp and keep moving, no matter where you're starting from. Life comes at all of us, whether you're running a company, chasing a dream, or just trying to get through the day. Some days, you need a kick to push forward; other days, a reminder to slow down and reset. This book gives you both—without the speeches. It's not meant to be read front to back. Flip through, find what hits, and apply it right away. Whether you're making big decisions or handling the day to day, this book is here to help you stay focused, stay in control, and keep leveling up.

It's easier to give advice
than to live by advice.

Whiskey
FOR THE SOUL

Have you ever noticed that people have the answer to every problem but their own? Try internalizing your advice to deal with your own problems, take your own solutions and see the outcome.

Celebrate All of Your Wins!

Whiskey
FOR THE SOUL

Big or small enjoy them all. Take a moment and enjoy the satisfaction of accomplishing a goal. Have a cookie, a shot of your favorite whiskey, or buy yourself something nice- just celebrate ALL of your wins.

Whiskey
FOR THE SOUL

It's not always what you do, it's sometimes what you DON'T DO.

Whiskey
FOR THE SOUL

When action is needed and you fail to respond, that inaction can be perceived as denial or abandonment. The silence can feel overwhelming and speaks louder than shouting 'NO' at the top of your lungs in the Grand Canyon.

Whiskey
FOR THE SOUL

Sometimes you've got to underthink and OVER-execute.

Procrastination comes in many forms. One of them is obsessing over minor details, like spending hours choosing a font but only writing one line. It's important to conceptualize your idea first and leave the finer details for later.

Whiskey
FOR THE SOUL

Make time to be alone, so you can connect and reflect on your thoughts.

Whiskey
FOR THE SOUL

We starve together, we EAT together.

Whiskey
FOR THE SOUL

Take time to de-clutter your mind. Life moves so fast between work, and loved ones, and passion, you need a moment to make sure YOU are ok.

Whiskey
FOR THE SOUL

One person brings the table, another brings the chairs, and everyone else contributes quality entrées, drinks, and sides. Then, we all eat. Too often, we expect one person to feed everyone, and while that can work, it takes a toll. Sharing the load not only makes the experience much more enjoyable, but also ensures it can happen more often

Whiskey
FOR THE SOUL

Now WHY would you do that?

Whiskey
FOR THE SOUL

The answer to this will have you double down on a great idea, reconsider a bad idea, and re-think an ok idea.

Whiskey
FOR THE SOUL

Don't just change-grow up.

Growth can be considered a form of change, depending on how you look at it. The change you're looking for might be found in redundant, consistent, repetition or development.

Whiskey
FOR THE SOUL

Did they make a million dollars selling books, or is the information in the book truly worth a million dollars?

Whiskey
FOR THE SOUL

Ever wonder if the people selling million-dollar advice are actually rich from the wisdom they share, or if they're just cashing in on a great sales pitch? Scammers or gurus-it can be hard to tell.

Whiskey
FOR THE SOUL

Don't compete CREATE.

Whiskey
FOR THE SOUL

Life isn't a competition; it's an experience, and you won't have your full experience focusing on someone else's life. YOU-versus-YOU everyday! Strive to be 1% better daily, focus on what you have to be and do, and leave love and gratitude for others as they live their experiences.

You can't save enough money. Make more.

Whiskey
FOR THE SOUL

Saved money loses value over time, invested money grows. Many keep their wealth in assets and investments, not liquid. How do you make your money circulate?

Whiskey FOR THE SOUL

Two traps to avoid; caring what they think and thinking that they care.

Whiskey
FOR THE SOUL

Opinions matter, but never let someone else's opinion or approval of you be the driving force of your choices or the main influence of your motives.

There's a big difference between risking it all, losing it all, and having nothing to lose.

Maybe... but a loss is a loss.

Happiness is taking the stairs and enjoying the climb.

Whiskey
FOR THE SOUL

Get lost in your passion! The work at times should reflect the same enjoyment as the feeling of completing a task or crushing a goal. Small successes along the way lead to the bigger ones we want to see in life.

Whiskey
FOR THE SOUL

If you think the price of winning is too high, wait 'til you get the bill for regret.

Whiskey
FOR THE SOUL

The experiences of trial, error, and success bring a thrill that's far more rewarding than merely acting without action. It feels great to dream, but it feels even better to achieve what felt impossible to achieve.

Whiskey
FOR THE SOUL

Driving faster doesn't make you less tired.

Whiskey
FOR THE SOUL

Speed won't get you there faster if you're running on empty. Sometimes a break or rest will make you more efficient for the next leg of the journey.

Whiskey
FOR THE SOUL

Shoot first - ask questions later.

Whiskey
FOR THE SOUL

Sometimes it's better to ask for forgiveness than permission. When I'm old, I want my stories to be full of 'Remember when's,' not 'What if's.' With a bit of logic, faith, and patience, you can achieve almost anything. And if it doesn't work out, at least you'll have **the best story at the next family dinner.**

Whiskey
FOR THE SOUL

How you see yourself is more important than how you're seen.

Whiskey
FOR THE SOUL

Your opinion of self and your knowledge of self means more than someone else's fleeting observation of you. WHO CARES what they think of you. What do YOU think of YOU?

Whiskey
FOR THE SOUL

Starve bad habits, feed good ones.

Forming good habits and giving them time and energy, is a great way to cancel out the bad ones. What you feed lives, what you starve dies.

Whiskey
FOR THE SOUL

Whatever you want to be great in will be a culmination of failure, resilience, heartbreak, and promise.

Whiskey
FOR THE SOUL

The work you put in will feel different on different days, even when you're doing what you love. There will be a range of emotions and life occurrences that come at different times, you might experience your highest high, and lowest low at the same time. But if you want to be great, work ethic will often times have to override feelings.

Whi
FOR

skey
HE SOUL

Whiskey
FOR THE SOUL

The path to success is the one you pave, and the materials you use to pave that road are the ones you have or have access to.

Whiskey
FOR THE SOUL

There's no magic formula, put in the work, barter the work, or pay for the work. No matter how you think it goes, the work that has to be done, has to be done, and that comes with a price, even if the currency is labor.

Most rich men think poor men are lazy. Most poor men think rich men are lucky.

Whiskey
FOR THE SOUL

Think about this in terms of assets. Now consider it in terms of family, relationships, friendships, health, and love. Is the rich man and the poor man the same or different in both scenarios?

Whiskey
FOR THE SOUL

Sometimes the weight you need to lose most isn't bodyweight.

Whiskey
FOR THE SOUL

Things, people, and situations can weigh you down and make life feel like you're toting an extra 50 pounds around with you. Try to examine the "weight" in your life.

Whiskey
FOR THE SOUL

Always business, always personal

Whiskey
FOR THE SOUL

In life, you'll work with people you don't like, and some won't like you. But don't let your ego cost you business or income. If you can respect the transaction—whether it's payment for a project or collaboration on a product —and the terms are clear, focus on getting it done

Knowledge isn't free; you have to pay attention.

Whiskey
FOR THE SOUL

Be aware of your experiences, your triggers, your bias, your TOXIC, what brings you joy, peace, and comfort. Knowledge-Of-Self is vital to success in every aspect of life.

Whiskey FOR THE SOUL

Listen to criticism, ignore praise

Whiskey
FOR THE SOUL

One will make you work harder, one will make you more comfortable. You don't have to take the criticism, but it gives you the opportunity to perfect the critique, and action is usually the best response.

Whiskey
FOR THE SOUL

When everyone is on the stage,
nobody is in the crowd.

Whiskey
FOR THE SOUL

If we don't give people honest and appropriate feedback, they will continue to operate under a false and potentially damaging assumption about their abilities. Some are built for the stage, some are built for the crowd, and everywhere in between.

Whiskey
FOR THE SOUL

Bet on the wave, not the surfer

Whiskey
FOR THE SOUL

Consistency wins more times than less.

Whiskey
FOR THE SOUL

Chasing pleasure is the sport of fools.

Whiskey
FOR THE SOUL

Always go with consistency, even when it's the tougher choice, unless you're gambling.

Whiskey
FOR THE SOUL

Before you beat a dog, find out who it's master is.

Whiskey
FOR THE SOUL

Simply put, pick your battles. Sometimes it's best to walk away, in this case RUN!

Whiskey FOR THE SOUL

When a clown moves into a palace it doesn't make him a king, it makes the castle a circus.

Whiskey
FOR THE SOUL

You might have bigger problems than you think.

Whiskey
FOR THE SOUL

A smile is a curve that sets everything straight.

Whiskey
FOR THE SOUL

When things get hectic or you're feeling overwhelmed, it's important to take a moment to get a handle on your mind and mood. Find something that makes you laugh or smile—a show, a comedy sketch, or a picture of someone you love. A simple smile can shift your entire outlook.

Whiskey
FOR THE SOUL

Have the courage to be disliked

Whiskey
FOR THE SOUL

Not everyone can see what you see. You might have to push forward alone at times-truthfully, most times. Colleagues, friends, clients, and customers may come and go, agree and disagree, but if you set the goal, don't waver.

Whiskey
FOR THE SOUL

A conversation about how you feel is not supposed to end in an argument

Whiskey
FOR THE SOUL

Stand on your opinion, double down! If they care, they'll hear.

Whiskey FOR THE SOUL

Get to it! Whatever YOU need to do is not going to get done if you don't do it.

Whiskey
FOR THE SOUL

No matter the task, you're either going to learn how to do it, pay someone to do it, or barter to get it done. Otherwise, make an effort to do one task a day that leads closer to your goal.

Whiskey
FOR THE SOUL

Facts over feelings

Whiskey
FOR THE SOUL

Feel how you feel, but don't ignore reality by living in your head. Most miscommunication starts with the gap between what was said and what you heard.

Whiskey
FOR THE SOUL

Impact may go unseen, but never unfelt.

Whiskey
FOR THE SOUL

They may not appreciate you now, but they will miss you when you're gone. Someone might forget what you said, but they won't forget how you make them feel.

Whiskey
FOR THE SOUL

Hard Times Make Hard Men, Hard Men Make Soft Times, Soft Times Make Soft Men, Soft Men Make Hard Times.

Whiskey
FOR THE SOUL

We create our world, but everyone does as well, and although you can establish what seems like a healthy environment and eco-system for you, it may have the reverse or adverse effect on others.

Whiskey
FOR THE SOUL

Grow through what you go through.

Whiskey
FOR THE SOUL

It's the circle of life. Don't let hard times stop you, learn from the failure, and use what you learn to get further along on the path.

Whiskey
FOR THE SOUL

Walk softly but leave a big footprint.

Be firm, but gentle when possible. Making a lasting impression is more about impact than volume.

Whiskey
FOR THE SOUL

Don't raise your voice, improve your argument.

Speaking louder doesn't make you right. In fact, the louder you talk, the less people tend to listen. Effective communication often requires strategy, not just raising your voice.

Whiskey
FOR THE SOUL

Some things are better left as thoughts.

Whiskey
FOR THE SOUL

Not everything is meant to be said, every time you have something to say. It's great to have an opinion, but it's really great to know when it doesn't matter.

Whiskey
FOR THE SOUL

A plan determines how your time is spent; the lack of a plan shows how your time is wasted.

Whiskey
FOR THE SOUL

Imagine your first or second time driving from New York to St. Louis solely on feelings, without GPS, you'd almost certainly get lost. Just like your journey needs a map, your time needs a plan.

Some people play the victim just to hide that they're the real villain.

People often mask their intentions until they get what they want, then their true motives are revealed.

Whiskey
FOR THE SOUL

If you fall down 8 times get up 9. If you fall down 98 times, get up 99.

Whiskey
FOR THE SOUL

Keep going, you got this.

Whiskey
FOR THE SOUL

Small successes along the way lead to the bigger ones we want to see in life

Whiskey
FOR THE SOUL

Success might seem to happen 'overnight,' but there are countless nights where it doesn't. Enjoy the process, nurture your passion, and when you add it all up, it's worth it.

Whiskey
FOR THE SOUL

Living The Lessons

By now, you've seen that life doesn't hand out favors. It's on you to make moves, adapt, and stay ahead. Whether you're leading in the boardroom, building from the ground up, or navigating everyday struggles, the game demands you stay sharp. No one's going to hand you anything—you've got to take it. This book isn't about giving you all the answers. Life doesn't come with a playbook. It's about showing you the mindset you need to keep pushing, even when the odds aren't in your favor. These pages are here to remind you that when challenges come, you don't retreat—you recalibrate, adjust, and step up. Every setback is an opportunity to rethink your next move. Success doesn't come to those who wait for the perfect moment. It comes to those who make their own opportunities, stay focused when others get distracted, and remain relentless in the pursuit of their vision. So, whenever life tests you, come back to these pages. Let them remind you: You have what it takes to keep moving forward. Confidence, control, and clarity—that's what wins the game. Keep that in mind, and you'll always be ready for what's next.

www.ingramcontent.com/pod-product-compliance
Lightning Source LLC
LaVergne TN
LVHW022328131224
799072LV00003B/471